50 Effortless Cooking Recipes for Home

By: Kelly Johnson

Table of Contents

- Spaghetti Aglio e Olio
- One-Pan Baked Lemon Garlic Chicken
- Vegetable Stir-Fry
- Caprese Salad
- Easy Margherita Pizza
- Baked Salmon with Dill
- Classic Grilled Cheese Sandwich
- Chicken Caesar Salad
- Shrimp Scampi Pasta
- Black Bean Quesadillas
- Greek Salad
- Teriyaki Chicken Skewers
- Roasted Vegetable Medley
- Tomato Basil Soup
- Lemon Herb Roasted Chicken Thighs
- Garlic Butter Shrimp
- Quinoa Salad with Chickpeas
- Beef and Broccoli Stir-Fry
- Pesto Pasta with Cherry Tomatoes
- Baked Ziti
- Honey Mustard Glazed Salmon
- Veggie Wrap with Hummus
- Margarita Chicken Tacos
- Lemon Garlic Butter Shrimp Pasta
- Caesar Pasta Salad
- Roasted Sweet Potato Wedges
- Teriyaki Salmon Bowl
- Spinach and Feta Stuffed Chicken Breast
- BBQ Pulled Chicken Sandwiches
- Egg Fried Rice
- One-Pot Chicken Alfredo
- Avocado Toast with Poached Egg
- Teriyaki Veggie Stir-Fry
- Lemon Butter Asparagus
- Chicken and Rice Casserole

- Mediterranean Chickpea Salad
- Baked Parmesan Crusted Tilapia
- Buffalo Chicken Wraps
- Caprese Chicken Skillet
- Sausage and Peppers Sheet Pan Dinner
- Zucchini Noodles with Pesto
- Cilantro Lime Chicken
- Ratatouille
- Broccoli Cheddar Stuffed Potatoes
- Turkey and Avocado Wrap
- Garlic Parmesan Roasted Brussels Sprouts
- Salsa Chicken
- Italian Sausage and White Bean Soup
- Cucumber Avocado Salad
- Lemon Rosemary Grilled Chicken Thighs

Spaghetti Aglio e Olio

Ingredients:

- 8 ounces (about 225g) spaghetti
- 4 cloves garlic, thinly sliced
- 1/2 teaspoon red pepper flakes (adjust to taste)
- 1/3 cup (80ml) extra-virgin olive oil
- Salt, to taste
- Black pepper, to taste
- Fresh parsley, chopped, for garnish
- Grated Parmesan cheese, for serving (optional)

Instructions:

Cook the Spaghetti: Bring a large pot of salted water to a boil. Cook the spaghetti according to the package instructions until al dente. Reserve about 1/2 cup of pasta cooking water and then drain the spaghetti.

Sauté Garlic and Red Pepper Flakes: While the pasta is cooking, heat the olive oil in a large skillet over medium heat. Add the thinly sliced garlic and red pepper flakes. Sauté until the garlic becomes golden, but be careful not to let it brown too much.

Combine Pasta and Garlic Oil: Add the drained spaghetti to the skillet with the garlic and oil. Toss to coat the pasta evenly with the garlic-infused oil. If the pasta seems dry, add a bit of the reserved pasta cooking water to achieve the desired consistency.

Season and Garnish: Season the dish with salt and black pepper to taste. Toss the spaghetti again to ensure even seasoning. Sprinkle chopped fresh parsley over the pasta for a burst of freshness.

Serve: Divide the Spaghetti Aglio e Olio among plates. Optionally, sprinkle with grated Parmesan cheese for added richness. Serve immediately and enjoy your delicious and effortless Italian pasta dish!

This recipe is quick to make, requiring just a few ingredients, and it allows the flavors of garlic and olive oil to shine.

One-Pan Baked Lemon Garlic Chicken

Ingredients:

- 4 boneless, skinless chicken breasts
- Salt and black pepper, to taste
- 3 tablespoons olive oil
- 4 cloves garlic, minced
- 1 teaspoon dried thyme
- 1 teaspoon dried rosemary
- 1 teaspoon paprika
- Zest of 1 lemon
- Juice of 1 lemon
- 1/2 cup (120ml) chicken broth
- Fresh parsley, chopped, for garnish

Instructions:

Preheat the Oven: Preheat your oven to 400°F (200°C).
Season the Chicken: Pat the chicken breasts dry with paper towels. Season them generously with salt and black pepper on both sides.
Sear the Chicken: In an oven-safe skillet, heat olive oil over medium-high heat. Sear the chicken breasts for about 2-3 minutes on each side, or until they develop a golden brown color.
Add Garlic and Herbs: Reduce the heat to medium. Add minced garlic, dried thyme, dried rosemary, and paprika to the skillet. Stir and cook for about 1 minute until the garlic is fragrant.
Add Lemon: Sprinkle lemon zest over the chicken and squeeze the juice of one lemon into the skillet.
Bake: Pour chicken broth into the skillet around the chicken. Transfer the skillet to the preheated oven and bake for approximately 20-25 minutes or until the chicken is cooked through, and its internal temperature reaches 165°F (74°C).
Garnish and Serve: Remove the skillet from the oven. Sprinkle chopped fresh parsley over the chicken for a burst of freshness. Serve the One-Pan Baked Lemon Garlic Chicken with your favorite sides, such as roasted vegetables, rice, or potatoes.

This dish is not only delicious but also convenient as it requires just one pan for both searing and baking, making cleanup a breeze. Enjoy your flavorful and easy-to-make lemon garlic chicken!

Vegetable Stir-Fry

Ingredients:

- 2 tablespoons vegetable oil
- 1 onion, thinly sliced
- 2 bell peppers (assorted colors), thinly sliced
- 1 carrot, julienned
- 1 zucchini, sliced
- 1 cup broccoli florets
- 1 cup snap peas, trimmed
- 3 cloves garlic, minced
- 1 tablespoon ginger, grated
- 3 tablespoons soy sauce
- 1 tablespoon oyster sauce
- 1 tablespoon sesame oil
- 1 tablespoon rice vinegar
- 1 teaspoon sugar
- 1 tablespoon cornstarch (optional, for thickening)
- Sesame seeds and green onions for garnish (optional)
- Cooked rice or noodles for serving

Instructions:

Prepare the Sauce: In a small bowl, whisk together soy sauce, oyster sauce, sesame oil, rice vinegar, and sugar. Set aside.
Stir-Fry Vegetables: Heat vegetable oil in a wok or a large skillet over medium-high heat. Add sliced onions and stir-fry for 1-2 minutes until they begin to soften.
Add Aromatics: Add minced garlic and grated ginger to the onions. Stir-fry for an additional 30 seconds until fragrant.
Cook Vegetables: Add bell peppers, carrot, zucchini, broccoli, and snap peas to the wok. Stir-fry for 4-5 minutes or until the vegetables are tender-crisp. Adjust the cooking time based on your preference for the crunchiness of the vegetables.
Combine with Sauce: Pour the prepared sauce over the vegetables in the wok. Toss everything together until the vegetables are well coated in the sauce.
Thicken (Optional): If you prefer a thicker sauce, mix cornstarch with a little water to create a slurry. Add it to the wok and stir well until the sauce thickens.

Serve: Remove the wok from heat. Serve the Vegetable Stir-Fry over cooked rice or noodles. Garnish with sesame seeds and chopped green onions if desired.

This Vegetable Stir-Fry is not only colorful and flavorful but also a great way to enjoy a variety of nutrient-packed vegetables. Feel free to customize the vegetables based on your preferences. Enjoy!

Caprese Salad

Ingredients:

- 4 large ripe tomatoes, sliced
- 8 ounces (about 225g) fresh mozzarella cheese, sliced
- Fresh basil leaves
- Extra-virgin olive oil
- Balsamic glaze (optional)
- Salt and black pepper, to taste

Instructions:

Slice Tomatoes and Mozzarella: Wash and slice the tomatoes and fresh mozzarella into approximately 1/4-inch thick slices.
Arrange on a Platter: Arrange the tomato and mozzarella slices alternately on a serving platter, creating a visually appealing pattern.
Add Basil Leaves: Tuck fresh basil leaves between the tomato and mozzarella slices. You can use whole leaves or chiffonade (thinly sliced) basil, depending on your preference.
Drizzle with Olive Oil: Drizzle extra-virgin olive oil over the salad. Use enough to add flavor but not so much that it overwhelms the dish.
Season with Salt and Pepper: Sprinkle salt and black pepper over the salad to taste. Keep in mind that the mozzarella can be a bit salty, so adjust accordingly.
Optional Balsamic Glaze: If you like, you can drizzle a balsamic glaze over the Caprese Salad for added sweetness and tanginess. Alternatively, you can use a balsamic reduction.
Serve: Serve the Caprese Salad immediately as a refreshing appetizer or side dish. It's best enjoyed when the ingredients are fresh.

Caprese Salad is a classic and elegant dish that showcases the wonderful combination of ripe tomatoes, creamy mozzarella, and aromatic basil. It's perfect for summer when these ingredients are at their peak freshness.

Easy Margherita Pizza

Ingredients:

- Pizza dough (store-bought or homemade)
- 1/2 cup pizza sauce (homemade or store-bought)
- 8 ounces fresh mozzarella cheese, sliced
- 2-3 large tomatoes, thinly sliced
- Fresh basil leaves
- Extra-virgin olive oil
- Salt and black pepper, to taste
- Cornmeal or flour, for dusting

Instructions:

Preheat the Oven: Preheat your oven to the highest temperature it can go (usually around 475-500°F or 245-260°C). If you have a pizza stone, place it in the oven during the preheating.

Prepare Pizza Dough: Roll out the pizza dough on a floured surface to your desired thickness. If you have a pizza peel, sprinkle it with cornmeal or flour to prevent sticking.

Assemble the Pizza: Transfer the rolled-out pizza dough to the pizza peel or a parchment paper-lined baking sheet. Spread the pizza sauce evenly over the dough, leaving a small border around the edges.

Add Mozzarella and Tomatoes: Place slices of fresh mozzarella evenly over the sauce. Arrange tomato slices on top. Season with salt and black pepper to taste.

Bake the Pizza: If using a pizza stone, carefully transfer the pizza (with parchment paper) onto the preheated stone in the oven. Otherwise, place the baking sheet directly into the oven. Bake for 10-12 minutes or until the crust is golden and the cheese is melted and bubbly.

Finish with Fresh Basil: Remove the pizza from the oven and immediately sprinkle fresh basil leaves over the hot pizza. Drizzle with extra-virgin olive oil for added flavor.

Slice and Serve: Let the Margherita Pizza cool for a minute or two before slicing. Slice and serve hot.

Enjoy the simplicity and deliciousness of homemade Margherita Pizza. It's a crowd-pleaser and perfect for a quick and satisfying meal.

Baked Salmon with Dill

Ingredients:

- 4 salmon fillets
- Salt and black pepper, to taste
- 2 tablespoons olive oil
- 2 tablespoons fresh dill, chopped
- 2 cloves garlic, minced
- 1 lemon, sliced
- Lemon zest (optional)
- 1 tablespoon Dijon mustard (optional)

Instructions:

Preheat the Oven: Preheat your oven to 375°F (190°C).
Prepare the Salmon: Pat the salmon fillets dry with paper towels. Season both sides with salt and black pepper.
Create Dill Mixture: In a small bowl, mix together olive oil, chopped fresh dill, minced garlic, and optional Dijon mustard.
Coat Salmon: Place the salmon fillets on a baking sheet lined with parchment paper or lightly greased. Brush the dill mixture over the top of each fillet, ensuring they are well coated.
Add Lemon Slices: Place lemon slices on top of each salmon fillet. Optionally, sprinkle lemon zest over the fillets for added flavor.
Bake: Bake in the preheated oven for about 15-20 minutes or until the salmon flakes easily with a fork. Cooking time may vary depending on the thickness of the fillets.
Serve: Once baked, remove the salmon from the oven. Serve the Baked Salmon with Dill hot, garnished with additional fresh dill if desired.

This simple and flavorful Baked Salmon with Dill is not only delicious but also packed with omega-3 fatty acids and other nutrients. Pair it with your favorite side dishes, such as roasted vegetables or a light salad, for a well-balanced meal.

Classic Grilled Cheese Sandwich

Ingredients:

- 4 slices of bread (white, whole wheat, or your choice)
- 8 slices of your favorite cheese (cheddar, American, Swiss, or a blend)
- Butter, softened
- Optional additions: ham, bacon, tomato slices, or caramelized onions

Instructions:

- Assemble the Sandwich:
    - Lay out four slices of bread.
    - Place two slices of cheese on two of the bread slices.
    - Add any optional ingredients you desire, such as ham, bacon, tomato slices, or caramelized onions.
    - Top with the remaining two slices of bread to form sandwiches.
- Butter the Bread:
    - Spread a thin layer of softened butter on one side of each sandwich.
- Heat the Pan:
    - Preheat a skillet or griddle over medium heat.
- Grill the Sandwiches:
    - Place the sandwiches, buttered side down, on the heated skillet or griddle.
    - Grill for 3-4 minutes on each side, or until the bread is golden brown, and the cheese is melted.
- Press if Desired:
    - If you have a panini press or a heavy skillet, you can press the sandwiches down gently while grilling to achieve a crispier texture.
- Serve:
    - Once the bread is golden brown and the cheese is melted, remove the sandwiches from the heat.
    - Allow them to cool for a minute, then slice diagonally if desired.
- Enjoy:
    - Serve your Classic Grilled Cheese Sandwiches hot and enjoy the gooey goodness!

Feel free to customize your grilled cheese with different types of bread and cheese to suit your preferences. It's a quick, simple, and comforting meal that's perfect for lunch or a quick dinner.

Chicken Caesar Salad

Ingredients:

For the Caesar Dressing:

- 1/2 cup mayonnaise
- 1/4 cup grated Parmesan cheese
- 2 tablespoons Dijon mustard
- 2 tablespoons freshly squeezed lemon juice
- 2 cloves garlic, minced
- 1 teaspoon Worcestershire sauce
- Salt and black pepper, to taste
- 1/3 cup extra-virgin olive oil

For the Salad:

- 2 boneless, skinless chicken breasts
- Salt and black pepper, to taste
- 1 tablespoon olive oil
- 1 large head of romaine lettuce, washed and chopped
- 1 cup croutons
- 1/4 cup grated Parmesan cheese (for topping)
- Lemon wedges (for garnish, optional)

Instructions:

Prepare the Caesar Dressing:
- In a bowl, whisk together mayonnaise, grated Parmesan, Dijon mustard, lemon juice, minced garlic, Worcestershire sauce, salt, and black pepper.
- Gradually whisk in the extra-virgin olive oil until the dressing is well combined and smooth. Set aside.

Cook the Chicken:
- Season the chicken breasts with salt and black pepper.
- In a skillet over medium-high heat, heat olive oil. Cook the chicken breasts for about 5-7 minutes per side or until cooked through and golden brown.
- Remove the chicken from the skillet and let it rest for a few minutes before slicing it into thin strips.

Assemble the Salad:

- In a large salad bowl, combine the chopped romaine lettuce, sliced grilled chicken, and croutons.

Add Dressing:
- Drizzle the Caesar dressing over the salad, tossing gently to coat all the ingredients.

Top with Parmesan:
- Sprinkle grated Parmesan cheese over the salad.

Serve:
- Divide the Chicken Caesar Salad onto individual plates.
- Garnish with lemon wedges if desired.

Optional Extras:
- Add extra toppings like cherry tomatoes, sliced cucumbers, or bacon bits for additional flavor and texture.

This Chicken Caesar Salad is a delicious and hearty meal that can be enjoyed for lunch or dinner. Customize it to your liking and savor the classic combination of flavors.

Shrimp Scampi Pasta

Ingredients:

- 8 ounces (about 225g) linguine or spaghetti
- 1 pound (about 450g) large shrimp, peeled and deveined
- Salt and black pepper, to taste
- 4 tablespoons unsalted butter
- 3 tablespoons olive oil
- 4 cloves garlic, minced
- 1/2 teaspoon red pepper flakes (adjust to taste)
- 1/4 cup dry white wine (optional)
- Zest of 1 lemon
- Juice of 1 lemon
- 1/4 cup fresh parsley, chopped
- Grated Parmesan cheese, for serving (optional)

Instructions:

Cook the Pasta:
- Cook the pasta in a large pot of salted boiling water according to the package instructions until al dente. Reserve about 1/2 cup of pasta cooking water before draining.

Prepare the Shrimp:
- Pat the shrimp dry with paper towels and season with salt and black pepper.

Sauté Shrimp:
- In a large skillet, heat 2 tablespoons of butter and 2 tablespoons of olive oil over medium-high heat. Add the shrimp to the skillet and cook for 1-2 minutes per side or until they turn pink. Remove the shrimp from the skillet and set aside.

Make the Sauce:
- In the same skillet, add the remaining 2 tablespoons of butter and 1 tablespoon of olive oil. Add minced garlic and red pepper flakes. Sauté for about 1 minute until the garlic is fragrant.

Deglaze with Wine (Optional):

- If using white wine, pour it into the skillet, scraping up any browned bits from the bottom of the pan. Allow it to simmer for 1-2 minutes to reduce slightly.

Combine with Pasta:
- Add the cooked and drained pasta to the skillet. Toss to coat the pasta in the garlic butter sauce.

Add Shrimp and Lemon:
- Gently stir in the cooked shrimp. Add lemon zest and lemon juice. Toss everything together until well combined.

Finish and Garnish:
- If needed, use some of the reserved pasta cooking water to adjust the consistency of the sauce. Stir in chopped fresh parsley. Taste and adjust the seasoning if necessary.

Serve:
- Divide the Shrimp Scampi Pasta among plates. Optionally, sprinkle with grated Parmesan cheese. Serve immediately.

Enjoy this Shrimp Scampi Pasta with its rich and flavorful combination of shrimp, garlic, and lemon. It's a perfect dish for a quick and satisfying meal.

Black Bean Quesadillas

Ingredients:

- 1 can (15 oz) black beans, drained and rinsed
- 1 cup corn kernels (fresh, frozen, or canned)
- 1 cup shredded cheese (cheddar, Monterey Jack, or a Mexican blend)
- 1/2 cup diced bell peppers (any color)
- 1/4 cup diced red onion
- 1 teaspoon ground cumin
- 1 teaspoon chili powder
- 1/2 teaspoon garlic powder
- Salt and pepper to taste
- 4 large flour tortillas
- Cooking spray or a small amount of vegetable oil for pan-frying

Optional toppings:

- Salsa
- Guacamole
- Sour cream
- Chopped cilantro
- Lime wedges

Instructions:

In a medium-sized bowl, combine the black beans, corn, shredded cheese, diced bell peppers, red onion, ground cumin, chili powder, garlic powder, salt, and pepper. Mix well to ensure all ingredients are evenly distributed.
Place a large skillet or frying pan over medium heat.
Lay out one tortilla and spoon a generous portion of the black bean mixture onto one half of the tortilla.
Fold the other half of the tortilla over the filling, creating a half-moon shape.
Lightly spray the skillet with cooking spray or add a small amount of vegetable oil.
Carefully place the filled tortilla in the skillet and cook for 2-3 minutes on each side, or until the tortilla is golden brown and the cheese is melted.
Repeat the process with the remaining tortillas and filling.

Once each quesadilla is cooked, transfer it to a cutting board and let it rest for a minute before slicing it into wedges.
Serve the black bean quesadillas with your choice of toppings, such as salsa, guacamole, sour cream, chopped cilantro, and lime wedges.

Enjoy your homemade black bean quesadillas! They make for a versatile and satisfying meal, suitable for lunch, dinner, or even as a tasty appetizer.

Greek Salad

Ingredients:

For the Salad:

- 4 cups chopped romaine lettuce or mixed salad greens
- 1 cucumber, diced
- 1 cup cherry tomatoes, halved
- 1 bell pepper (any color), sliced
- 1/2 red onion, thinly sliced
- 1/2 cup Kalamata olives, pitted
- 1/2 cup crumbled feta cheese
- Optional: 1/4 cup chopped fresh parsley

For the Dressing:

- 1/4 cup extra virgin olive oil
- 2 tablespoons red wine vinegar
- 1 teaspoon dried oregano
- Salt and pepper to taste

Instructions:

In a large salad bowl, combine the chopped romaine lettuce, cucumber, cherry tomatoes, bell pepper, red onion, Kalamata olives, and feta cheese.
If desired, sprinkle chopped fresh parsley over the salad.
In a small bowl, whisk together the extra virgin olive oil, red wine vinegar, dried oregano, salt, and pepper to make the dressing.
Drizzle the dressing over the salad and toss gently to coat the ingredients evenly.
Serve immediately, or refrigerate for a short time if you prefer a chilled salad.

This Greek salad is a vibrant and tasty option that showcases the delicious flavors of Mediterranean cuisine. Enjoy it as a side dish or add grilled chicken or shrimp to make it a complete meal.

Teriyaki Chicken Skewers

Ingredients:

For the Teriyaki Marinade:

- 1/2 cup soy sauce
- 1/4 cup mirin (sweet rice wine)
- 2 tablespoons sake (or white wine)
- 2 tablespoons brown sugar
- 1 tablespoon honey
- 2 cloves garlic, minced
- 1 teaspoon ginger, grated
- 1 tablespoon sesame oil (optional)
- 1.5 lbs (about 700g) boneless, skinless chicken thighs, cut into bite-sized pieces

For the Skewers:

- Bamboo skewers (soaked in water for at least 30 minutes to prevent burning)
- Optional: Sliced green onions and sesame seeds for garnish

Instructions:

In a bowl, whisk together all the teriyaki marinade ingredients until the sugar is dissolved.

Place the chicken pieces in a shallow dish or a zip-top bag and pour about half of the teriyaki marinade over the chicken. Reserve the other half for basting and serving.

Marinate the chicken in the refrigerator for at least 30 minutes to 2 hours, allowing the flavors to infuse.

Preheat your grill or oven to medium-high heat.

Thread the marinated chicken pieces onto the soaked skewers.

If grilling, oil the grates lightly to prevent sticking. Grill the chicken skewers for about 5-7 minutes per side or until cooked through, basting with the reserved marinade.

If baking, preheat your oven to 400°F (200°C) and place the skewers on a lined baking sheet. Bake for approximately 15-20 minutes or until the chicken is fully cooked, turning and basting halfway through.

Garnish the teriyaki chicken skewers with sliced green onions and sesame seeds if desired.

Serve the skewers over steamed rice or with your favorite side dishes.

These teriyaki chicken skewers are savory, slightly sweet, and make for a delightful meal. Enjoy the delicious flavors of homemade teriyaki!

Roasted Vegetable Medley

Ingredients:

- 3 cups mixed vegetables, chopped into bite-sized pieces (e.g., bell peppers, zucchini, cherry tomatoes, red onion, carrots, broccoli, cauliflower)
- 2 tablespoons olive oil
- 2 cloves garlic, minced
- 1 teaspoon dried thyme
- 1 teaspoon dried rosemary
- Salt and pepper to taste
- Optional: Balsamic vinegar or grated Parmesan cheese for serving

Instructions:

Preheat your oven to 425°F (220°C).
In a large mixing bowl, combine the chopped vegetables.
In a small bowl, whisk together the olive oil, minced garlic, dried thyme, dried rosemary, salt, and pepper.
Pour the olive oil mixture over the vegetables and toss until the vegetables are evenly coated.
Spread the vegetables in a single layer on a baking sheet lined with parchment paper or a silicone baking mat.
Roast in the preheated oven for 20-25 minutes or until the vegetables are tender and slightly caramelized, stirring once or twice during cooking to ensure even roasting.
Remove the roasted vegetable medley from the oven and let it cool for a few minutes.
Optionally, drizzle balsamic vinegar over the roasted vegetables or sprinkle them with grated Parmesan cheese before serving.
Serve the roasted vegetable medley as a side dish alongside your favorite main course.

Feel free to experiment with different herbs and spices based on your taste preferences. This roasted vegetable medley is not only delicious but also a colorful and nutritious addition to your meal.

Tomato Basil Soup

Ingredients:

- 2 tablespoons olive oil
- 1 onion, chopped
- 2 cloves garlic, minced
- 2 cans (28 oz each) whole peeled tomatoes
- 1 can (14 oz) crushed tomatoes
- 1 teaspoon sugar (optional, to balance acidity)
- 1 cup vegetable broth
- 1/2 cup fresh basil leaves, chopped
- Salt and pepper to taste
- 1/2 cup heavy cream or coconut milk (optional, for a creamy version)
- Grated Parmesan cheese for garnish (optional)
- Fresh basil leaves for garnish (optional)

Instructions:

In a large pot, heat the olive oil over medium heat. Add the chopped onion and cook until softened, about 5 minutes.
Add the minced garlic and cook for an additional 1-2 minutes until fragrant.
Pour in the whole peeled tomatoes, crushed tomatoes, and vegetable broth. If using whole tomatoes, break them apart with a spoon.
Add the sugar (if using) to balance the acidity of the tomatoes. Season with salt and pepper to taste.
Bring the soup to a simmer and let it cook for about 15-20 minutes to allow the flavors to meld.
Stir in the chopped fresh basil and cook for an additional 5 minutes.
If you prefer a creamy tomato basil soup, use an immersion blender to blend the soup until smooth. Alternatively, transfer the soup to a blender in batches and blend until smooth. Be cautious when blending hot liquids.
Return the soup to the pot and stir in the heavy cream or coconut milk if using. Heat through but do not boil.
Taste and adjust the seasoning if needed.
Serve the tomato basil soup hot, garnished with grated Parmesan cheese and fresh basil leaves if desired.

Enjoy this comforting and flavorful tomato basil soup on its own or with a side of crusty bread.

Lemon Herb Roasted Chicken Thighs

Ingredients:

- 6 bone-in, skin-on chicken thighs
- 2 lemons, juiced and zest of one lemon
- 3 tablespoons olive oil
- 3 cloves garlic, minced
- 1 tablespoon fresh thyme leaves (or 1 teaspoon dried thyme)
- 1 tablespoon fresh rosemary, chopped (or 1 teaspoon dried rosemary)
- Salt and black pepper to taste
- Optional: 1 teaspoon paprika for added color and flavor

Instructions:

Preheat your oven to 400°F (200°C).

In a small bowl, whisk together the lemon juice, lemon zest, olive oil, minced garlic, thyme, rosemary, salt, pepper, and paprika if using.

Pat the chicken thighs dry with paper towels and place them in a large bowl or a resealable plastic bag.

Pour the lemon herb marinade over the chicken thighs, making sure they are well coated. You can marinate the chicken for at least 30 minutes for more flavor, but you can also cook it immediately if you're short on time.

Place the marinated chicken thighs on a baking sheet lined with parchment paper or a greased baking dish, skin side up.

Roast the chicken in the preheated oven for 35-40 minutes or until the internal temperature reaches 165°F (74°C) and the skin is golden and crispy.

If desired, broil the chicken for an additional 2-3 minutes at the end to get a more golden and crispy skin.

Remove the chicken from the oven and let it rest for a few minutes before serving.

Serve the lemon herb roasted chicken thighs with your favorite side dishes.

This dish is not only simple to prepare but also incredibly flavorful. The combination of lemon and herbs creates a bright and aromatic profile that enhances the natural taste of the chicken. Enjoy your delicious and juicy lemon herb roasted chicken thighs!

Garlic Butter Shrimp

Ingredients:

- 1 pound large shrimp, peeled and deveined
- 3 tablespoons unsalted butter
- 4 cloves garlic, minced
- 1 teaspoon paprika
- 1/2 teaspoon red pepper flakes (adjust to taste)
- Salt and black pepper to taste
- 2 tablespoons fresh parsley, chopped
- 1 tablespoon lemon juice (optional)

Instructions:

In a large skillet, melt the butter over medium-high heat.
Add the minced garlic to the melted butter and sauté for about 1-2 minutes until fragrant. Be careful not to burn the garlic.
Add the shrimp to the skillet in a single layer. Season with paprika, red pepper flakes, salt, and black pepper.
Cook the shrimp for 2-3 minutes on one side until they start to turn pink.
Flip the shrimp and continue cooking for an additional 2-3 minutes until fully cooked. The shrimp should be opaque and slightly browned on both sides.
Stir in chopped fresh parsley and lemon juice if using, and cook for an additional 1-2 minutes.
Taste and adjust the seasoning if needed.
Remove the skillet from heat and serve the garlic butter shrimp immediately.
Garnish with additional fresh parsley and lemon wedges if desired.

Serve the garlic butter shrimp over pasta, rice, or with a side of crusty bread to soak up the delicious buttery sauce. This quick and flavorful dish is sure to become a favorite for seafood lovers.

Quinoa Salad with Chickpeas

Ingredients:

For the Salad:

- 1 cup quinoa, rinsed and cooked according to package instructions
- 1 can (15 oz) chickpeas, drained and rinsed
- 1 cucumber, diced
- 1 bell pepper (any color), diced
- 1 cup cherry tomatoes, halved
- 1/4 cup red onion, finely chopped
- 1/4 cup fresh parsley, chopped
- 1/4 cup feta cheese, crumbled (optional)

For the Dressing:

- 3 tablespoons extra virgin olive oil
- 2 tablespoons lemon juice
- 1 teaspoon Dijon mustard
- 1 clove garlic, minced
- Salt and black pepper to taste

Instructions:

Cook the quinoa according to the package instructions. Once cooked, let it cool to room temperature.
In a large bowl, combine the cooked quinoa, chickpeas, diced cucumber, diced bell pepper, cherry tomatoes, chopped red onion, and fresh parsley.
If using, add the crumbled feta cheese to the bowl.
In a small bowl, whisk together the extra virgin olive oil, lemon juice, Dijon mustard, minced garlic, salt, and black pepper to create the dressing.
Pour the dressing over the quinoa and chickpea mixture. Toss everything together until well combined and evenly coated with the dressing.
Taste the salad and adjust the seasoning if needed.
Chill the quinoa salad in the refrigerator for at least 30 minutes before serving to allow the flavors to meld.

Before serving, give the salad a gentle toss and garnish with additional fresh parsley or feta cheese if desired.

This quinoa salad with chickpeas is not only delicious but also packed with protein, fiber, and various nutrients. Enjoy it as a light and satisfying meal on its own or as a side dish to complement your main course.

Beef and Broccoli Stir-Fry

Ingredients:

For the Marinade:

- 1 lb (450g) flank steak, thinly sliced against the grain
- 2 tablespoons soy sauce
- 1 tablespoon oyster sauce
- 1 tablespoon cornstarch
- 1 tablespoon rice vinegar or white vinegar
- 1 teaspoon sesame oil
- 1 teaspoon sugar
- 2 cloves garlic, minced
- 1 teaspoon fresh ginger, grated

For the Stir-Fry:

- 2 tablespoons vegetable oil, divided
- 4 cups broccoli florets
- 1/2 cup beef broth or water
- 3 tablespoons soy sauce
- 1 tablespoon oyster sauce
- 1 tablespoon hoisin sauce
- 1 tablespoon cornstarch mixed with 2 tablespoons water (for thickening)
- Sesame seeds for garnish (optional)
- Cooked rice for serving

Instructions:

In a bowl, combine the thinly sliced flank steak with the soy sauce, oyster sauce, cornstarch, rice vinegar, sesame oil, sugar, minced garlic, and grated ginger. Let it marinate for at least 15-30 minutes.

Heat 1 tablespoon of vegetable oil in a large wok or skillet over medium-high heat.

Add the marinated beef slices to the hot pan and stir-fry for 2-3 minutes or until browned. Remove the beef from the pan and set it aside.

In the same pan, add another tablespoon of vegetable oil.
Add the broccoli florets and stir-fry for 2-3 minutes until they start to turn bright green and are slightly tender.
Pour in the beef broth or water and cover the pan with a lid. Let the broccoli steam for an additional 2-3 minutes until it reaches the desired tenderness.
Return the cooked beef to the pan with the broccoli.
In a small bowl, mix together the soy sauce, oyster sauce, and hoisin sauce. Pour this sauce over the beef and broccoli, stirring to coat everything evenly.
In a small bowl, mix the cornstarch with water to create a slurry. Pour it into the pan and stir to thicken the sauce.
Continue cooking for an additional 1-2 minutes until the sauce is thickened and coats the beef and broccoli.
Garnish with sesame seeds if desired.
Serve the beef and broccoli stir-fry over cooked rice.

Enjoy this homemade beef and broccoli stir-fry that's both delicious and much healthier than takeout.

Pesto Pasta with Cherry Tomatoes

Ingredients:

- 8 oz (about 225g) pasta of your choice (e.g., spaghetti, fettuccine, or penne)
- 1 cup fresh basil leaves, packed
- 1/3 cup grated Parmesan cheese
- 1/3 cup pine nuts or walnuts
- 2 cloves garlic, peeled
- 1/2 cup extra-virgin olive oil
- Salt and black pepper to taste
- 1 cup cherry tomatoes, halved
- Grated Parmesan cheese for serving (optional)

Instructions:

Cook the pasta according to the package instructions until al dente. Drain and set aside.
In a food processor, combine the fresh basil, grated Parmesan cheese, pine nuts or walnuts, and garlic cloves.
Pulse the ingredients until finely chopped.
With the food processor running, slowly pour in the extra-virgin olive oil until the mixture forms a smooth pesto sauce. Season with salt and black pepper to taste.
In a large bowl, toss the cooked pasta with the freshly made pesto sauce until the pasta is well coated.
Add the halved cherry tomatoes to the pasta and toss gently to distribute them evenly.
If desired, sprinkle additional grated Parmesan cheese on top before serving.
Serve the pesto pasta with cherry tomatoes warm or at room temperature.

This dish is not only vibrant and flavorful but also customizable. Feel free to add grilled chicken, shrimp, or your favorite vegetables to enhance the dish further. Enjoy your delicious homemade pesto pasta with cherry tomatoes!

Baked Ziti

Ingredients:

- 1 lb (about 450g) ziti pasta
- 1 tablespoon olive oil
- 1 onion, finely chopped
- 2 cloves garlic, minced
- 1 lb (about 450g) ground beef or Italian sausage
- 1 can (28 oz) crushed tomatoes
- 1 can (15 oz) tomato sauce
- 1 teaspoon dried oregano
- 1 teaspoon dried basil
- Salt and black pepper to taste
- 2 cups ricotta cheese
- 2 cups shredded mozzarella cheese
- 1/2 cup grated Parmesan cheese
- Fresh basil or parsley for garnish (optional)

Instructions:

Preheat your oven to 375°F (190°C). Grease a 9x13-inch baking dish.
Cook the ziti pasta according to the package instructions until al dente. Drain and set aside.
In a large skillet, heat the olive oil over medium heat. Add the chopped onion and sauté until softened.
Add the minced garlic and cook for an additional 1-2 minutes until fragrant.
Add the ground beef or Italian sausage to the skillet, breaking it apart with a spoon. Cook until browned and cooked through. Drain any excess fat.
Stir in the crushed tomatoes, tomato sauce, dried oregano, dried basil, salt, and black pepper. Simmer the sauce for about 10-15 minutes to allow the flavors to meld.
In a large bowl, mix together the cooked ziti pasta, ricotta cheese, and half of the shredded mozzarella.
Spread a thin layer of the meat sauce on the bottom of the prepared baking dish.
Layer half of the ziti mixture on top of the sauce, followed by half of the remaining meat sauce.
Repeat the layers, finishing with a layer of meat sauce on top.

Sprinkle the remaining shredded mozzarella and grated Parmesan cheese over the top.

Cover the baking dish with aluminum foil and bake in the preheated oven for 25 minutes.

Remove the foil and bake for an additional 10-15 minutes or until the cheese is melted and bubbly.

Allow the baked ziti to rest for a few minutes before serving. Garnish with fresh basil or parsley if desired.

Serve the baked ziti with a side of garlic bread or a simple green salad for a delicious and comforting meal.

Honey Mustard Glazed Salmon

Ingredients:

- 4 salmon fillets (about 6 oz each)
- Salt and black pepper to taste
- 2 tablespoons Dijon mustard
- 2 tablespoons whole grain mustard
- 2 tablespoons honey
- 1 tablespoon soy sauce
- 1 tablespoon olive oil
- 2 cloves garlic, minced
- 1 teaspoon fresh ginger, grated (optional)
- Lemon wedges for serving
- Chopped fresh parsley for garnish (optional)

Instructions:

Preheat your oven to 400°F (200°C). Line a baking sheet with parchment paper or lightly grease it.

Season the salmon fillets with salt and black pepper to taste. Place them on the prepared baking sheet, skin side down.

In a small bowl, whisk together the Dijon mustard, whole grain mustard, honey, soy sauce, olive oil, minced garlic, and grated ginger (if using).

Brush the honey mustard glaze over the tops of the salmon fillets, ensuring they are evenly coated.

Bake the salmon in the preheated oven for 12-15 minutes or until the salmon is cooked through and easily flakes with a fork.

If desired, you can broil the salmon for an additional 2-3 minutes at the end to caramelize the glaze and add a bit of crispiness to the top.

Remove the salmon from the oven and let it rest for a couple of minutes.

Serve the honey mustard glazed salmon on a platter, drizzle with any remaining glaze from the baking sheet, and garnish with chopped fresh parsley if desired.

Serve with lemon wedges on the side for an extra burst of freshness.

Enjoy your honey mustard glazed salmon with your favorite side dishes, such as steamed vegetables, rice, or quinoa. It's a flavorful and healthy option for a quick and satisfying meal.

Veggie Wrap with Hummus

Ingredients:

- 4 whole wheat or spinach tortillas
- 1 cup hummus (store-bought or homemade)
- 1 cup shredded carrots
- 1 cucumber, thinly sliced
- 1 bell pepper (any color), thinly sliced
- 1 cup cherry tomatoes, halved
- 1/2 red onion, thinly sliced
- 1 cup mixed greens (spinach, kale, or lettuce)
- Feta cheese crumbles (optional)
- Kalamata olives, pitted and sliced (optional)
- Balsamic glaze or vinaigrette (optional)
- Salt and black pepper to taste

Instructions:

Lay out the tortillas on a clean surface.

Spread a generous layer of hummus onto each tortilla, leaving a small border around the edges.

Evenly distribute the shredded carrots, cucumber slices, bell pepper slices, cherry tomato halves, red onion slices, and mixed greens onto each tortilla.

If using, sprinkle feta cheese crumbles and sliced Kalamata olives over the veggies.

Drizzle a small amount of balsamic glaze or vinaigrette over the veggies for added flavor (optional).

Season with salt and black pepper to taste.

Carefully fold in the sides of each tortilla and then roll it up tightly from the bottom, creating a wrap.

If desired, secure the wraps with toothpicks or wrap them in parchment paper to hold their shape.

Slice the wraps in half diagonally before serving.

Enjoy these Veggie Wraps with Hummus as a nutritious and satisfying meal. They're versatile, and you can customize them with your favorite vegetables and additional toppings for added flavor.

Margarita Chicken Tacos

Ingredients:

For the Margarita Chicken:

- 1.5 lbs (about 680g) boneless, skinless chicken thighs
- 1/4 cup tequila
- 1/4 cup fresh lime juice
- 2 tablespoons orange juice
- 2 tablespoons olive oil
- 2 cloves garlic, minced
- 1 teaspoon ground cumin
- 1 teaspoon chili powder
- 1 teaspoon dried oregano
- Salt and black pepper to taste

For the Tacos:

- Corn or flour tortillas
- Shredded lettuce or cabbage
- Diced tomatoes
- Sliced red onion
- Fresh cilantro, chopped
- Avocado slices or guacamole
- Lime wedges for serving

Instructions:

In a bowl, whisk together the tequila, fresh lime juice, orange juice, olive oil, minced garlic, ground cumin, chili powder, dried oregano, salt, and black pepper to create the marinade.

Place the chicken thighs in a resealable plastic bag or shallow dish. Pour the margarita marinade over the chicken, making sure it's well-coated. Marinate in the refrigerator for at least 30 minutes, or ideally, up to 4 hours.

Preheat your grill or grill pan over medium-high heat.

Remove the chicken from the marinade and grill for about 5-7 minutes per side or until the chicken is fully cooked and has nice grill marks. Cooking time may vary depending on the thickness of the chicken thighs.

Once cooked, let the chicken rest for a few minutes before slicing it into strips. Warm the tortillas according to the package instructions.

Assemble the tacos by placing sliced margarita chicken on each tortilla. Top with shredded lettuce or cabbage, diced tomatoes, sliced red onion, chopped cilantro, and avocado slices or guacamole.

Serve the margarita chicken tacos with lime wedges on the side for squeezing over the top.

These Margarita Chicken Tacos are fresh, vibrant, and bursting with citrusy and savory flavors. They're perfect for a casual dinner or a festive gathering. Enjoy!

Lemon Garlic Butter Shrimp Pasta

Ingredients:

- 8 oz (about 225g) linguine or your favorite pasta
- 1 lb (about 450g) large shrimp, peeled and deveined
- Salt and black pepper to taste
- 3 tablespoons unsalted butter, divided
- 4 cloves garlic, minced
- Zest of 1 lemon
- Juice of 1 lemon
- 1/2 cup chicken broth or white wine
- 1/2 teaspoon red pepper flakes (optional, for a bit of heat)
- 1/4 cup fresh parsley, chopped
- Grated Parmesan cheese for serving

Instructions:

Cook the pasta according to the package instructions until al dente. Reserve about 1/2 cup of pasta cooking water before draining.
Season the shrimp with salt and black pepper.
In a large skillet, melt 2 tablespoons of butter over medium-high heat. Add the shrimp and cook for 1-2 minutes per side or until they turn pink and opaque. Remove the shrimp from the skillet and set them aside.
In the same skillet, add the remaining 1 tablespoon of butter. Add minced garlic and sauté for about 30 seconds until fragrant.
Pour in the chicken broth or white wine to deglaze the pan, scraping up any browned bits from the bottom.
Add the lemon zest, lemon juice, and red pepper flakes (if using). Simmer for 2-3 minutes to allow the flavors to meld.
Return the cooked shrimp to the skillet and toss to coat them in the lemon garlic butter sauce.
Add the cooked pasta to the skillet, tossing to combine and coat the pasta in the flavorful sauce. If needed, use the reserved pasta cooking water to loosen the sauce.
Stir in the chopped parsley and continue tossing until everything is well combined.
Season with additional salt and black pepper to taste.

Serve the lemon garlic butter shrimp pasta hot, garnished with grated Parmesan cheese.

Enjoy this delightful and zesty lemon garlic butter shrimp pasta as a quick and satisfying meal. It's perfect for busy weeknights or a special dinner occasion.

Caesar Pasta Salad

Ingredients:

For the Salad:

- 8 oz (about 225g) rotini or your favorite pasta
- 2 cups chopped romaine lettuce
- 1 cup cherry tomatoes, halved
- 1/2 cup black olives, sliced
- 1/2 cup croutons
- 1/4 cup grated Parmesan cheese

For the Caesar Dressing:

- 1/2 cup mayonnaise
- 1/4 cup grated Parmesan cheese
- 2 tablespoons Dijon mustard
- 2 tablespoons lemon juice
- 2 cloves garlic, minced
- 1 teaspoon anchovy paste (optional)
- Salt and black pepper to taste

Instructions:

Cook the pasta according to the package instructions until al dente. Drain and let it cool to room temperature.

In a large bowl, combine the cooked pasta, chopped romaine lettuce, cherry tomatoes, black olives, croutons, and grated Parmesan cheese.

In a separate bowl, whisk together the mayonnaise, grated Parmesan cheese, Dijon mustard, lemon juice, minced garlic, anchovy paste (if using), salt, and black pepper. Adjust the seasoning to taste.

Pour the Caesar dressing over the pasta salad and toss until all the ingredients are well coated.

Refrigerate the Caesar pasta salad for at least 30 minutes before serving to allow the flavors to meld.

Before serving, toss the salad again to ensure the dressing is evenly distributed.

Garnish with additional grated Parmesan cheese and croutons if desired.

This Caesar pasta salad is a great side dish for barbecues, picnics, or a light lunch. You can also add grilled chicken or shrimp for extra protein to turn it into a complete meal. Enjoy the refreshing and classic flavors of Caesar salad combined with the heartiness of pasta!

Roasted Sweet Potato Wedges

Ingredients:

- 2 large sweet potatoes, peeled and cut into wedges
- 2 tablespoons olive oil
- 1 teaspoon smoked paprika
- 1 teaspoon garlic powder
- 1 teaspoon onion powder
- 1/2 teaspoon ground cumin
- 1/2 teaspoon ground cinnamon
- Salt and black pepper to taste
- Optional: Fresh parsley, chopped, for garnish

Instructions:

Preheat your oven to 425°F (220°C). Line a baking sheet with parchment paper for easy cleanup.

In a large bowl, combine the sweet potato wedges with olive oil, smoked paprika, garlic powder, onion powder, ground cumin, ground cinnamon, salt, and black pepper. Toss until the sweet potato wedges are evenly coated.

Spread the seasoned sweet potato wedges in a single layer on the prepared baking sheet, ensuring they are not crowded to allow for even roasting.

Roast in the preheated oven for 25-30 minutes or until the sweet potatoes are tender and golden brown, flipping them halfway through the cooking time for even browning.

Remove the sweet potato wedges from the oven and let them rest for a couple of minutes.

Optional: Garnish with chopped fresh parsley for a burst of freshness.

Serve the roasted sweet potato wedges as a side dish alongside your favorite main course.

These roasted sweet potato wedges are perfect for a healthy and flavorful side dish. They make a great addition to your meals, providing a balance of sweetness and savory spices. Enjoy!

Teriyaki Salmon Bowl

Ingredients:

For Teriyaki Salmon:

- 4 salmon fillets
- 1/4 cup soy sauce
- 2 tablespoons mirin (Japanese sweet rice wine)
- 2 tablespoons sake (or white wine)
- 2 tablespoons brown sugar
- 1 tablespoon honey
- 1 teaspoon grated ginger
- 2 cloves garlic, minced
- Sesame seeds for garnish (optional)
- Sliced green onions for garnish (optional)

For the Bowl:

- 2 cups cooked rice (white or brown)
- Sliced avocado
- Shredded carrots
- Sliced cucumber
- Edamame beans (steamed)
- Nori strips (seaweed strips)
- Sesame seeds for garnish
- Sliced green onions for garnish
- Soy sauce for drizzling

Instructions:

Preheat your oven to 400°F (200°C).
In a small saucepan, combine soy sauce, mirin, sake, brown sugar, honey, grated ginger, and minced garlic. Bring the mixture to a simmer over medium heat, stirring occasionally, until the sugar dissolves and the sauce thickens slightly. Remove from heat.
Place the salmon fillets on a baking sheet lined with parchment paper or greased foil.
Brush the salmon fillets generously with the prepared teriyaki sauce, reserving some for serving.
Bake in the preheated oven for about 12-15 minutes or until the salmon is cooked through and flakes easily with a fork.

While the salmon is baking, prepare the rice and gather your desired toppings. Once the salmon is done, remove it from the oven and brush with additional teriyaki sauce.

Assemble the bowls by placing a portion of rice in each bowl, topping it with teriyaki salmon, and arranging the sliced avocado, shredded carrots, sliced cucumber, edamame beans, and nori strips around the salmon.

Drizzle with additional teriyaki sauce, sprinkle with sesame seeds and sliced green onions.

Serve the teriyaki salmon bowls immediately, with extra soy sauce on the side if desired.

Enjoy this flavorful and nutritious teriyaki salmon bowl that combines the richness of salmon with the savory and sweet notes of teriyaki sauce, complemented by a variety of fresh and vibrant toppings.

Spinach and Feta Stuffed Chicken Breast

Ingredients:

- 4 boneless, skinless chicken breasts
- Salt and black pepper to taste
- 1 tablespoon olive oil
- 2 cups fresh spinach, chopped
- 1/2 cup feta cheese, crumbled
- 1/4 cup sun-dried tomatoes, chopped (optional)
- 2 cloves garlic, minced
- 1 teaspoon dried oregano
- 1 teaspoon dried basil
- 1 teaspoon paprika
- Toothpicks or kitchen twine (for securing the chicken)

Instructions:

Preheat your oven to 375°F (190°C).
Season the chicken breasts with salt and black pepper.
In a skillet, heat olive oil over medium heat. Add chopped spinach and garlic, and sauté until the spinach wilts and the garlic is fragrant.
Remove the skillet from the heat and stir in the crumbled feta cheese, sun-dried tomatoes (if using), dried oregano, dried basil, and paprika. Mix until well combined.
Butterfly each chicken breast by making a horizontal cut along one side, being careful not to cut all the way through. Open the chicken breasts like a book.
Divide the spinach and feta mixture evenly among the chicken breasts, placing it on one side of each butterflied breast.
Fold the other side of the chicken breast over the filling, creating a stuffed chicken breast. Secure the edges with toothpicks or tie with kitchen twine.
Season the stuffed chicken breasts with a bit more salt, pepper, and paprika.
Heat an oven-safe skillet over medium-high heat. Add a bit of olive oil.
Place the stuffed chicken breasts in the skillet and sear for 2-3 minutes on each side until golden brown.
Transfer the skillet to the preheated oven and bake for 20-25 minutes or until the chicken is cooked through.
Remove the toothpicks or kitchen twine before serving.

Serve the spinach and feta stuffed chicken breast with your favorite side dishes, such as roasted vegetables, quinoa, or a fresh salad. Enjoy this flavorful and impressive dish!

BBQ Pulled Chicken Sandwiches

Ingredients:

For the BBQ Pulled Chicken:

- 4 boneless, skinless chicken breasts
- 1 cup barbecue sauce (homemade or your favorite store-bought brand)
- 1/2 cup chicken broth
- 2 tablespoons apple cider vinegar
- 2 tablespoons brown sugar
- 1 tablespoon Dijon mustard
- 1 teaspoon smoked paprika
- 1 teaspoon garlic powder
- 1 teaspoon onion powder
- Salt and black pepper to taste

For Assembling the Sandwiches:

- Hamburger buns or sandwich rolls
- Coleslaw (optional, for topping)
- Pickles (optional, for serving)

Instructions:

In a bowl, whisk together the barbecue sauce, chicken broth, apple cider vinegar, brown sugar, Dijon mustard, smoked paprika, garlic powder, onion powder, salt, and black pepper. This is your barbecue sauce mixture.
Place the chicken breasts in a slow cooker or crockpot. Pour the barbecue sauce mixture over the chicken.
Cook the chicken on low for 6-8 hours or on high for 3-4 hours, or until the chicken is tender and easily shreds.
Once the chicken is cooked, use two forks to shred it directly in the slow cooker, allowing it to absorb the flavorful sauce.
Toast the hamburger buns or sandwich rolls.
Spoon the pulled chicken onto the bottom half of each bun.

Optionally, top the pulled chicken with coleslaw for a crunchy and refreshing contrast.
Place the top half of the bun on the coleslaw and press down gently.
Serve the BBQ pulled chicken sandwiches with pickles on the side.

These BBQ pulled chicken sandwiches are perfect for a casual meal or a gathering. The tender and flavorful pulled chicken pairs wonderfully with the sweetness and smokiness of the barbecue sauce. Enjoy!

Egg Fried Rice

Ingredients:

- 3 cups cooked jasmine or long-grain rice (preferably cold, leftover rice)
- 2 tablespoons vegetable oil
- 2 eggs, lightly beaten
- 1 cup mixed vegetables (peas, carrots, corn, and/or diced bell peppers)
- 3 green onions, chopped
- 3 tablespoons soy sauce
- 1 tablespoon oyster sauce (optional)
- 1 teaspoon sesame oil
- Salt and black pepper to taste

Instructions:

Preparation: Ensure that the cooked rice is cold or at least at room temperature. This helps to prevent the rice from sticking together during the frying process. You can use leftover rice from a previous meal or cook it in advance and allow it to cool.

Vegetables: If using frozen mixed vegetables, thaw them before cooking. If using fresh vegetables, dice them into small, uniform pieces.

Cooking Process:
- Heat vegetable oil in a large wok or skillet over medium-high heat.
- Add the mixed vegetables and stir-fry for 2-3 minutes until they are tender-crisp. Push the vegetables to one side of the pan.

Eggs:
- Pour the beaten eggs into the other side of the pan. Allow them to cook for a moment without stirring.
- Once the eggs start to set, scramble them with a spatula until they are fully cooked.

Combine:
- Mix the cooked vegetables with the scrambled eggs in the pan.

Rice:
- Add the cold or room temperature cooked rice to the pan. Break up any clumps with the spatula and stir-fry to combine the ingredients evenly.

Seasoning:

- Pour soy sauce and oyster sauce (if using) over the rice. Stir well to ensure even distribution of the sauces.
- Drizzle sesame oil over the rice and continue to stir-fry.

Final Adjustments:
- Season with salt and black pepper to taste.
- Add chopped green onions and stir them into the fried rice.

Serve:
- Once everything is well combined and heated through, remove the pan from heat.
- Serve the egg fried rice hot, garnished with additional green onions if desired.

Feel free to customize this basic egg fried rice recipe by adding proteins like cooked chicken, shrimp, or tofu. It's a versatile dish that's great as a side or a complete meal on its own. Enjoy your homemade egg fried rice!

One-Pot Chicken Alfredo

Ingredients:

- 1 lb (about 450g) fettuccine pasta
- 2 tablespoons unsalted butter
- 1 lb (about 450g) boneless, skinless chicken breasts, cut into bite-sized pieces
- Salt and black pepper to taste
- 3 cloves garlic, minced
- 4 cups chicken broth
- 1 cup heavy cream
- 1 cup grated Parmesan cheese
- 1 cup shredded mozzarella cheese
- 1 teaspoon dried Italian herbs (optional)
- Fresh parsley, chopped, for garnish

Instructions:

Cooking the Chicken:
- In a large pot or Dutch oven, melt the butter over medium heat.
- Season the chicken pieces with salt and black pepper.
- Add the chicken to the pot and cook until browned on all sides. Remove the chicken from the pot and set it aside.

Sautéing Garlic:
- In the same pot, add minced garlic and sauté for about 30 seconds until fragrant.

Cooking Pasta:
- Pour in the chicken broth and bring it to a boil.
- Add the fettuccine pasta, ensuring it's submerged in the liquid.
- Cook the pasta according to the package instructions, stirring occasionally to prevent sticking.

Creating Alfredo Sauce:
- Once the pasta is cooked, reduce the heat to low.
- Add the cooked chicken back to the pot.
- Pour in the heavy cream, grated Parmesan cheese, shredded mozzarella cheese, and dried Italian herbs (if using).
- Stir continuously until the cheeses melt and the sauce thickens, creating a creamy Alfredo sauce.

Final Adjustments:

- Season with additional salt and black pepper to taste.
- Garnish with chopped fresh parsley.

Serve:
- Serve the one-pot chicken Alfredo hot, either in the pot or transferred to a serving dish.

This one-pot chicken Alfredo is not only delicious but also makes cleanup a breeze. Feel free to customize the recipe by adding vegetables like spinach, broccoli, or peas for extra color and nutrition. Enjoy your comforting and creamy chicken Alfredo!

Avocado Toast with Poached Egg

Ingredients:

- 2 slices whole-grain bread (or your preferred bread)
- 1 ripe avocado
- 2 large eggs
- Salt and black pepper to taste
- Red pepper flakes (optional, for a bit of heat)
- Lemon wedges (optional, for serving)
- Fresh herbs, such as chopped cilantro or chives (optional, for garnish)

Instructions:

Toast the Bread:
- Toast the slices of bread to your liking. You can use a toaster, toaster oven, or a regular oven.

Prepare the Avocado:
- While the bread is toasting, cut the ripe avocado in half and remove the pit. Scoop the avocado flesh into a bowl.

Mash the Avocado:
- Mash the avocado with a fork until you achieve your desired level of creaminess. You can leave it slightly chunky or make it smooth.

Season the Avocado:
- Season the mashed avocado with salt and black pepper to taste. Optionally, add a pinch of red pepper flakes for some heat.

Poach the Eggs:
- Poach the eggs using your preferred method. A common method is to bring a pot of water to a gentle simmer, add a splash of vinegar, and carefully slide the cracked eggs into the simmering water. Cook for about 3-4 minutes for a runny yolk.

Assemble the Avocado Toast:
- Spread the mashed avocado evenly over the toasted bread slices.

Add the Poached Eggs:
- Carefully place a poached egg on top of each avocado-covered toast.

Season and Garnish:
- Sprinkle a bit more salt and black pepper on top of the poached eggs. Optionally, garnish with fresh herbs like chopped cilantro or chives.

Serve:
- Serve the avocado toast with poached eggs immediately, with lemon wedges on the side if desired.

This avocado toast with a poached egg is a delicious combination of creamy avocado and a perfectly cooked egg, offering a balance of flavors and textures. It makes for a wholesome breakfast or a light and satisfying meal at any time of the day. Enjoy!

Teriyaki Veggie Stir-Fry

Ingredients:

For the Teriyaki Sauce:

- 1/4 cup soy sauce
- 2 tablespoons water
- 2 tablespoons mirin (Japanese sweet rice wine)
- 1 tablespoon honey
- 1 teaspoon sesame oil
- 1 teaspoon cornstarch

For the Stir-Fry:

- 1 tablespoon vegetable oil
- 1 bell pepper, thinly sliced
- 1 carrot, julienned or thinly sliced
- 1 zucchini, thinly sliced
- 1 cup broccoli florets
- 1 cup snap peas, trimmed
- 2 cloves garlic, minced
- 1 tablespoon fresh ginger, grated
- 1 cup firm tofu, cubed (optional)
- Cooked rice or noodles for serving

Instructions:

Prepare the Teriyaki Sauce:
- In a small bowl, whisk together the soy sauce, water, mirin, honey, sesame oil, and cornstarch until the cornstarch is dissolved. Set aside.

Prepare the Tofu (if using):
- If using tofu, press it between paper towels to remove excess moisture. Cut it into cubes.

Stir-Fry:
- Heat vegetable oil in a wok or large skillet over medium-high heat.

Cook the Vegetables:

- Add the bell pepper, carrot, zucchini, broccoli, and snap peas to the hot wok. Stir-fry for 3-4 minutes or until the vegetables are crisp-tender.

Add Garlic and Ginger:
- Add the minced garlic and grated ginger to the vegetables. Stir-fry for an additional 1-2 minutes until fragrant.

Add Tofu (if using):
- If using tofu, add the cubes to the wok and cook for 2-3 minutes until lightly browned.

Pour in Teriyaki Sauce:
- Pour the prepared teriyaki sauce over the vegetables (and tofu) in the wok. Stir well to coat the vegetables evenly.

Simmer:
- Allow the sauce to simmer for 2-3 minutes, or until it thickens and coats the vegetables.

Serve:
- Serve the teriyaki veggie stir-fry over cooked rice or noodles.

Garnish (Optional):
- Garnish with sesame seeds or chopped green onions if desired.

Enjoy your homemade teriyaki veggie stir-fry! This versatile dish can be easily customized by adding your favorite vegetables or protein sources. It's a tasty and nutritious option for a quick and satisfying meal.

Lemon Butter Asparagus

Ingredients:

- 1 bunch of asparagus, woody ends trimmed
- 2 tablespoons unsalted butter
- 2 cloves garlic, minced
- Zest of 1 lemon
- 2 tablespoons fresh lemon juice
- Salt and black pepper to taste
- Optional: Parmesan cheese, grated, for serving

Instructions:

Blanch the Asparagus:
- Bring a large pot of salted water to a boil. Add the trimmed asparagus and cook for 2-3 minutes, or until they are bright green and slightly tender but still crisp. Immediately transfer the asparagus to a bowl of ice water to stop the cooking process. Drain and set aside.

Sauté the Asparagus:
- In a large skillet or pan, melt the butter over medium heat.
- Add the minced garlic and sauté for about 1 minute until fragrant, being careful not to let it brown.

Add Asparagus:
- Add the blanched asparagus to the skillet, tossing to coat them in the garlic butter.

Seasoning:
- Pour in the fresh lemon juice and sprinkle the lemon zest over the asparagus. Toss again to combine.
- Season with salt and black pepper to taste. Adjust the seasoning as needed.

Finish and Serve:
- Cook the asparagus in the lemon butter sauce for an additional 2-3 minutes, or until they are heated through and well-coated with the flavors.

Optional Garnish:
- Optionally, sprinkle grated Parmesan cheese over the asparagus just before serving.

Serve Hot:

- Transfer the lemon butter asparagus to a serving platter or individual plates.

This Lemon Butter Asparagus is a simple and elegant side dish that pairs well with a variety of main courses. It's a perfect addition to your spring and summer meals. Enjoy!

Chicken and Rice Casserole

Ingredients:

- 1.5 lbs (about 680g) boneless, skinless chicken breasts, cut into bite-sized pieces
- 1 cup long-grain white rice
- 2 cups chicken broth
- 1 cup frozen peas and carrots mix
- 1/2 cup diced onion
- 1/2 cup diced celery
- 1/2 cup diced bell pepper (any color)
- 2 cloves garlic, minced
- 1 teaspoon dried thyme
- 1 teaspoon dried oregano
- 1/2 teaspoon paprika
- Salt and black pepper to taste
- 1 cup shredded cheddar cheese
- 1/2 cup grated Parmesan cheese
- 1/4 cup chopped fresh parsley (optional, for garnish)

Instructions:

Preheat the Oven:
- Preheat your oven to 375°F (190°C).

Cook the Chicken:
- Season the chicken pieces with salt, black pepper, dried thyme, dried oregano, and paprika.
- In a large oven-safe skillet or casserole dish, brown the chicken over medium heat until cooked through. Remove the cooked chicken from the skillet and set it aside.

Sauté Vegetables:
- In the same skillet, add a bit of oil if needed. Sauté the diced onion, celery, and bell pepper until they are softened.

Add Rice and Garlic:
- Add the rice and minced garlic to the skillet. Cook for 1-2 minutes, stirring frequently.

Combine Ingredients:
- Pour in the chicken broth and bring the mixture to a simmer.

- Add the frozen peas and carrots mix, cooked chicken, shredded cheddar cheese, and grated Parmesan cheese. Stir until well combined.

Bake:
- Cover the skillet or casserole dish with a lid or aluminum foil.
- Transfer the dish to the preheated oven and bake for about 25-30 minutes, or until the rice is cooked and the liquid is absorbed.

Finish and Garnish:
- If desired, uncover the casserole for the last 5 minutes of baking to allow the top to brown slightly.
- Garnish with chopped fresh parsley before serving.

Serve:
- Serve the chicken and rice casserole hot, directly from the skillet or casserole dish.

This chicken and rice casserole is a complete and comforting meal in one dish. Feel free to customize it with your favorite vegetables or add herbs and spices to suit your taste. Enjoy!

Mediterranean Chickpea Salad

Ingredients:

For the Salad:

- 2 cans (15 oz each) chickpeas, drained and rinsed
- 1 cucumber, diced
- 1 cup cherry tomatoes, halved
- 1/2 red onion, finely chopped
- 1/2 cup Kalamata olives, pitted and sliced
- 1/2 cup crumbled feta cheese
- 1/4 cup fresh parsley, chopped
- 1/4 cup fresh mint, chopped (optional)

For the Dressing:

- 1/4 cup extra-virgin olive oil
- 2 tablespoons red wine vinegar
- 1 clove garlic, minced
- 1 teaspoon dried oregano
- Salt and black pepper to taste
- Lemon wedges for serving (optional)

Instructions:

Prepare the Chickpeas:
- Drain and rinse the chickpeas thoroughly. If you have time, you can also cook dried chickpeas.

Assemble the Salad:
- In a large salad bowl, combine the chickpeas, diced cucumber, cherry tomatoes, finely chopped red onion, sliced Kalamata olives, crumbled feta cheese, fresh parsley, and optional chopped mint.

Prepare the Dressing:
- In a small bowl, whisk together the extra-virgin olive oil, red wine vinegar, minced garlic, dried oregano, salt, and black pepper.

Dress the Salad:

- Pour the dressing over the chickpea salad and toss gently to ensure all ingredients are well coated.

Chill:
- Refrigerate the Mediterranean chickpea salad for at least 30 minutes to allow the flavors to meld.

Serve:
- Before serving, give the salad a final toss. Optionally, garnish with additional fresh herbs.
- Serve chilled with lemon wedges on the side for squeezing over individual servings, if desired.

This Mediterranean chickpea salad is not only delicious but also packed with protein and fiber. It makes for a great side dish or a light and satisfying main course. Enjoy the vibrant flavors of the Mediterranean in every bite!

Baked Parmesan Crusted Tilapia

Ingredients:

- 4 tilapia fillets
- 1/2 cup grated Parmesan cheese
- 1/4 cup breadcrumbs (plain or Italian-seasoned)
- 1 teaspoon dried oregano
- 1 teaspoon dried parsley
- 1/2 teaspoon garlic powder
- 1/2 teaspoon onion powder
- 1/2 teaspoon paprika
- Salt and black pepper to taste
- 2 tablespoons melted butter
- Lemon wedges for serving

Instructions:

Preheat the Oven:
- Preheat your oven to 425°F (220°C). Line a baking sheet with parchment paper or lightly grease it.

Prepare the Parmesan Coating:
- In a shallow bowl, combine the grated Parmesan cheese, breadcrumbs, dried oregano, dried parsley, garlic powder, onion powder, paprika, salt, and black pepper. Mix well.

Coat the Tilapia:
- Pat the tilapia fillets dry with paper towels.
- Brush each fillet with melted butter on both sides.

Dredge in Parmesan Mixture:
- Press each tilapia fillet into the Parmesan mixture, coating both sides evenly and pressing the coating onto the fish.

Place on Baking Sheet:
- Place the coated tilapia fillets on the prepared baking sheet.

Bake:
- Bake in the preheated oven for 12-15 minutes, or until the tilapia is cooked through and the crust is golden brown.

Broil (Optional):

- If you want a crispier crust, you can broil the tilapia for an additional 1-2 minutes, but keep a close eye to prevent burning.

Serve:
- Remove the baked Parmesan-crusted tilapia from the oven and let it rest for a minute.
- Serve the tilapia fillets with lemon wedges on the side for squeezing over the top.

This baked Parmesan-crusted tilapia is a quick and flavorful dish that pairs well with your favorite side dishes, such as steamed vegetables, rice, or a fresh salad. Enjoy the crispy, cheesy goodness!

Buffalo Chicken Wraps

Ingredients:

For Buffalo Chicken:

- 1 lb boneless, skinless chicken breasts, cooked and shredded
- 1/2 cup buffalo sauce
- 2 tablespoons unsalted butter, melted
- 1 teaspoon garlic powder
- Salt and black pepper to taste

For Wraps:

- Large tortillas (flour or whole wheat)
- Shredded lettuce
- Diced tomatoes
- Sliced red onion
- Crumbled blue cheese or ranch dressing
- Avocado slices (optional)

Instructions:

Prepare Buffalo Chicken:
- In a bowl, mix the shredded chicken with buffalo sauce, melted butter, garlic powder, salt, and black pepper. Ensure the chicken is well-coated with the buffalo sauce mixture.

Assemble the Wraps:
- Lay out the tortillas on a clean surface.

Add Fillings:
- Place a portion of the buffalo chicken mixture in the center of each tortilla.

Layer Vegetables:
- Top the chicken with shredded lettuce, diced tomatoes, sliced red onion, crumbled blue cheese (or drizzle with ranch dressing), and avocado slices if using.

Wrap and Roll:

- Fold the sides of the tortilla over the fillings, and then roll it up tightly from the bottom to create a wrap.

Serve:
- Slice each wrap in half diagonally and secure with toothpicks if needed.
- Serve the buffalo chicken wraps immediately, and enjoy!

These buffalo chicken wraps are perfect for a quick lunch or dinner, and you can customize them with your favorite toppings. The combination of spicy buffalo chicken, crisp vegetables, and creamy dressing creates a flavor-packed and satisfying meal.

Caprese Chicken Skillet

Ingredients:

- 4 boneless, skinless chicken breasts
- Salt and black pepper to taste
- 2 tablespoons olive oil
- 4 cloves garlic, minced
- 1 pint cherry or grape tomatoes, halved
- 8 oz fresh mozzarella, sliced
- Fresh basil leaves, for garnish
- Balsamic glaze, for drizzling

Instructions:

Preheat the Oven:
- Preheat your oven to 400°F (200°C).

Season Chicken:
- Season the chicken breasts with salt and black pepper on both sides.

Sear the Chicken:
- In an oven-safe skillet, heat olive oil over medium-high heat. Sear the chicken breasts for 2-3 minutes on each side, or until they develop a golden brown crust.

Add Garlic and Tomatoes:
- Add minced garlic to the skillet and sauté for about 30 seconds until fragrant. Add the halved cherry tomatoes to the skillet.

Bake:
- Transfer the skillet to the preheated oven and bake for 15-20 minutes, or until the chicken is cooked through.

Add Mozzarella:
- Remove the skillet from the oven. Place slices of fresh mozzarella on top of each chicken breast.

Broil (Optional):
- If you want the mozzarella to be golden and bubbly, you can place the skillet under the broiler for 1-2 minutes. Keep a close eye to prevent burning.

Garnish:
- Garnish the Caprese chicken with fresh basil leaves.

Drizzle with Balsamic Glaze:

- Drizzle the chicken and tomatoes with balsamic glaze just before serving. Serve:
- Serve the Caprese chicken directly from the skillet. Optionally, serve it over a bed of cooked pasta or alongside a salad.

This Caprese chicken skillet is a simple and elegant dish that captures the essence of the classic Caprese salad. The combination of juicy tomatoes, creamy mozzarella, and fragrant basil elevates the flavor of the tender chicken breasts. Enjoy this delightful and visually appealing meal!

Sausage and Peppers Sheet Pan Dinner

Ingredients:

- 1 lb Italian sausage links (sweet or spicy), sliced
- 1 red bell pepper, sliced
- 1 yellow bell pepper, sliced
- 1 green bell pepper, sliced
- 1 large onion, sliced
- 3 tablespoons olive oil
- 1 teaspoon dried oregano
- 1 teaspoon dried thyme
- 1 teaspoon garlic powder
- Salt and black pepper to taste
- Fresh parsley, chopped, for garnish (optional)

Instructions:

Preheat the Oven:
- Preheat your oven to 400°F (200°C).

Prepare Ingredients:
- In a large bowl, combine the sliced sausage, sliced bell peppers, and sliced onion.

Season:
- Drizzle olive oil over the sausage and peppers mixture. Sprinkle dried oregano, dried thyme, garlic powder, salt, and black pepper. Toss everything together until the ingredients are well coated.

Arrange on a Sheet Pan:
- Spread the seasoned sausage, peppers, and onions on a large, rimmed baking sheet in an even layer.

Bake:
- Bake in the preheated oven for 25-30 minutes, or until the sausage is cooked through, and the peppers and onions are tender. You can stir the ingredients halfway through the cooking time for even roasting.

Garnish:
- If desired, garnish the sausage and peppers with chopped fresh parsley before serving.

Serve:

- Serve the sausage and peppers straight from the sheet pan. Optionally, you can serve it over cooked rice, pasta, or with crusty bread.

This sheet pan sausage and peppers dinner is not only flavorful but also requires minimal cleanup, making it a perfect weeknight meal. The combination of savory sausage and sweet, roasted peppers is a classic and satisfying pairing. Enjoy your easy and delicious sheet pan dinner!

Zucchini Noodles with Pesto

Ingredients:

- 4 medium-sized zucchini, spiralized into noodles
- 1 cup fresh basil leaves, packed
- 1/2 cup grated Parmesan cheese
- 1/3 cup pine nuts
- 2 cloves garlic
- 1/2 cup extra-virgin olive oil
- Salt and pepper to taste
- Optional: Cherry tomatoes, sliced for garnish

Instructions:

Prepare the Zucchini Noodles:
- Wash and trim the ends of the zucchini.
- Use a spiralizer to create zucchini noodles.
- If you don't have a spiralizer, you can use a vegetable peeler to create ribbon-like strips.

Make the Pesto:
- In a food processor, combine the fresh basil, grated Parmesan cheese, pine nuts, and garlic.
- Pulse until the ingredients are finely chopped.

Add Olive Oil:
- With the food processor running, slowly drizzle in the olive oil until the pesto reaches your desired consistency.

Season:
- Season the pesto with salt and pepper to taste. Adjust the quantities based on your preference.

Combine:
- In a large bowl, toss the zucchini noodles with the freshly made pesto until the noodles are well coated.

Serve:
- Divide the zucchini noodles onto plates and garnish with additional grated Parmesan cheese.
- If desired, add sliced cherry tomatoes on top for a burst of color and freshness.

Enjoy:
- Serve the zucchini noodles with pesto immediately while they are still fresh and vibrant.

Feel free to customize this recipe by adding grilled chicken, shrimp, or other vegetables for extra protein and nutrients. It's a versatile and low-carb option that's perfect for a light and satisfying meal.

Cilantro Lime Chicken

Ingredients:

- 4 boneless, skinless chicken breasts
- 1/4 cup fresh lime juice (about 2 limes)
- 3 tablespoons olive oil
- 3 cloves garlic, minced
- 1 teaspoon ground cumin
- 1 teaspoon chili powder
- 1/2 teaspoon paprika
- Salt and black pepper to taste
- 1/4 cup fresh cilantro, chopped
- Lime wedges for serving

Instructions:

Marinate the Chicken:
- In a bowl, whisk together lime juice, olive oil, minced garlic, cumin, chili powder, paprika, salt, and black pepper.

Prepare the Chicken:
- Place the chicken breasts in a resealable plastic bag or shallow dish.
- Pour the marinade over the chicken, ensuring it is well-coated.
- Seal the bag or cover the dish and let it marinate in the refrigerator for at least 30 minutes. For more flavor, you can marinate it for a few hours or overnight.

Cook the Chicken:
- Preheat your grill or grill pan over medium-high heat.
- Remove the chicken from the marinade, allowing any excess to drip off.
- Grill the chicken for about 6-8 minutes per side or until it reaches an internal temperature of 165°F (74°C).

Rest and Garnish:
- Once cooked, let the chicken rest for a few minutes before slicing.
- Garnish the chicken with chopped cilantro.

Serve:
- Serve the cilantro lime chicken slices with lime wedges on the side for an extra burst of citrus flavor.

Optional Sides:

- This dish pairs well with rice, quinoa, or a side of roasted vegetables. You can also serve it in tacos, salads, or wraps.

Enjoy the bright and fresh flavors of cilantro and lime in this easy-to-make chicken dish. It's a versatile recipe that can be adapted to your taste preferences and works well for both casual dinners and special occasions.

Ratatouille

Ingredients:

- 1 eggplant, sliced into 1/4-inch rounds
- 2 zucchinis, sliced into 1/4-inch rounds
- 1 yellow bell pepper, sliced
- 1 red bell pepper, sliced
- 1 large onion, thinly sliced
- 4 tomatoes, sliced
- 4 cloves garlic, minced
- 2 tablespoons tomato paste
- 2 tablespoons olive oil
- 1 teaspoon dried thyme
- 1 teaspoon dried rosemary
- Salt and pepper to taste
- Fresh basil or parsley for garnish

Instructions:

Preheat the Oven:
- Preheat your oven to 375°F (190°C).

Prepare the Vegetables:
- Arrange the sliced eggplant, zucchini, bell peppers, and tomatoes in a concentric pattern in a large oven-safe baking dish. You can layer them or arrange them in rows, alternating the vegetables.

Make the Sauce:
- In a small bowl, mix together minced garlic, tomato paste, olive oil, dried thyme, dried rosemary, salt, and pepper.

Coat the Vegetables:
- Drizzle the sauce over the arranged vegetables, ensuring they are well-coated.

Bake:
- Cover the baking dish with foil and bake in the preheated oven for about 45-50 minutes, or until the vegetables are tender.

Garnish and Serve:
- Remove the foil and bake for an additional 10-15 minutes to allow the top to lightly brown.

- Garnish with fresh basil or parsley before serving.

Serve:
- Ratatouille can be served on its own as a vegetarian main dish or as a side dish. It pairs well with crusty bread, pasta, rice, or quinoa.

This ratatouille recipe is a great way to showcase the vibrant flavors of fresh vegetables. It's a versatile dish that can be enjoyed on its own or paired with other dishes, and it's perfect for those looking to incorporate more vegetables into their meals.

Broccoli Cheddar Stuffed Potatoes

Ingredients:

- 4 large baking potatoes
- 2 cups broccoli florets, steamed or blanched
- 1 1/2 cups shredded cheddar cheese
- 1/2 cup sour cream
- 2 tablespoons butter
- Salt and pepper to taste
- Optional toppings: chopped green onions, crispy bacon bits

Instructions:

Bake the Potatoes:
- Preheat your oven to 400°F (200°C).
- Wash the potatoes thoroughly and prick them with a fork. Place them directly on the oven rack or on a baking sheet.
- Bake for about 45-60 minutes, or until the potatoes are tender when pierced with a fork.

Prepare the Broccoli:
- While the potatoes are baking, steam or blanch the broccoli until it's tender but still vibrant green. Set aside.

Cut and Scoop:
- Once the potatoes are done, let them cool slightly. Cut a thin slice off the top of each potato.
- Carefully scoop out the flesh from each potato into a mixing bowl, leaving a thin layer of potato inside the skin to create a sturdy shell.

Mash and Mix:
- Mash the scooped-out potato flesh in the bowl.
- Add butter, sour cream, salt, and pepper. Mix until creamy and well combined.

Stuff the Potatoes:
- Fold in the steamed broccoli and 1 cup of shredded cheddar cheese into the mashed potato mixture.
- Stuff the potato shells with the broccoli-cheddar filling.

Bake Again:
- Sprinkle the remaining 1/2 cup of cheddar cheese on top of each stuffed potato.

- Place the stuffed potatoes back in the oven and bake for an additional 10-15 minutes, or until the cheese is melted and bubbly.

Serve:
- Remove the stuffed potatoes from the oven, and let them cool for a few minutes.
- Garnish with optional toppings such as chopped green onions or crispy bacon bits before serving.

These Broccoli Cheddar Stuffed Potatoes make for a satisfying and comforting meal. They can be served as a main dish or a side, and they're sure to be a hit with anyone who enjoys the classic combination of broccoli and cheddar.

Turkey and Avocado Wrap

Ingredients:

- 1 large tortilla or wrap of your choice
- 4-6 slices of roasted turkey breast
- 1 ripe avocado, sliced
- 1/2 cup shredded lettuce
- 1/4 cup diced tomatoes
- 1/4 cup sliced red onions
- 1/4 cup shredded cheese (cheddar, Monterey Jack, or your favorite)
- 2 tablespoons mayonnaise
- 1 tablespoon Dijon mustard
- Salt and pepper to taste

Instructions:

Lay the tortilla or wrap on a clean surface.
In the center of the wrap, layer the roasted turkey slices.
Add the sliced avocado on top of the turkey.
Sprinkle shredded lettuce, diced tomatoes, and sliced red onions over the turkey and avocado.
In a small bowl, mix together mayonnaise and Dijon mustard. Spread the mixture evenly over the ingredients in the wrap.
Sprinkle shredded cheese over the top.
Season with salt and pepper to taste.
Carefully fold in the sides of the tortilla and then roll it up tightly from the bottom, creating a wrap.
If you prefer, you can secure the wrap with toothpicks or wrap it in parchment paper for easier handling.
Slice the wrap in half diagonally, and it's ready to serve!

Feel free to customize the wrap with your favorite additional ingredients or condiments. Enjoy your Turkey and Avocado Wrap!

Garlic Parmesan Roasted Brussels Sprouts

Ingredients:

- 1 pound Brussels sprouts, trimmed and halved
- 2 tablespoons olive oil
- 3 cloves garlic, minced
- 1/3 cup grated Parmesan cheese
- Salt and pepper to taste
- Optional: Red pepper flakes for a bit of heat
- Optional: Fresh lemon wedges for serving

Instructions:

Preheat your oven to 400°F (200°C).

In a large bowl, toss the halved Brussels sprouts with olive oil, minced garlic, salt, and pepper until the Brussels sprouts are evenly coated.

Spread the Brussels sprouts in a single layer on a baking sheet lined with parchment paper or a silicone baking mat.

Roast in the preheated oven for about 20-25 minutes, or until the Brussels sprouts are golden brown and crispy on the edges. Shake or stir them halfway through the cooking time for even roasting.

Remove the Brussels sprouts from the oven and immediately sprinkle the grated Parmesan cheese over them. Toss the Brussels sprouts to coat them evenly with the cheese while they are still hot.

If desired, add red pepper flakes for a bit of heat.

Transfer the Garlic Parmesan Roasted Brussels Sprouts to a serving dish and serve immediately.

Optionally, serve with fresh lemon wedges on the side for a citrusy touch.

This dish makes for a flavorful and satisfying side. Enjoy your Garlic Parmesan Roasted Brussels Sprouts!

Salsa Chicken

Ingredients:

- 4 boneless, skinless chicken breasts
- 1 cup salsa (use your favorite variety)
- 1 cup shredded cheddar or Mexican blend cheese
- 1 teaspoon cumin
- 1 teaspoon chili powder
- 1/2 teaspoon garlic powder
- 1/2 teaspoon onion powder
- Salt and pepper to taste
- Fresh cilantro or green onions for garnish (optional)

Instructions:

Preheat your oven to 375°F (190°C).
Season the chicken breasts with cumin, chili powder, garlic powder, onion powder, salt, and pepper. Make sure to coat both sides evenly.
Place the seasoned chicken breasts in a baking dish.
Pour the salsa over the chicken breasts, making sure to cover them evenly.
Bake in the preheated oven for about 25-30 minutes or until the chicken is cooked through. The internal temperature should reach 165°F (74°C).
In the last 5 minutes of baking, sprinkle the shredded cheese over the chicken to melt and get bubbly.
Once the chicken is fully cooked and the cheese is melted, remove the baking dish from the oven.
Garnish with fresh cilantro or green onions if desired.
Serve the salsa chicken over rice, quinoa, or with your favorite side dishes.

This salsa chicken is quick, easy, and packed with flavor. Feel free to customize the recipe by adding toppings like diced tomatoes, avocado, or a dollop of sour cream. Enjoy your delicious salsa chicken!

Italian Sausage and White Bean Soup

Ingredients:

- 1 lb (about 450g) Italian sausage, casings removed (you can use sweet or spicy, based on your preference)
- 1 tablespoon olive oil
- 1 large onion, finely chopped
- 3 cloves garlic, minced
- 2 carrots, peeled and diced
- 2 celery stalks, diced
- 4 cups chicken broth
- 2 cans (15 oz each) white beans (cannellini or Great Northern), drained and rinsed
- 1 can (14 oz) diced tomatoes, undrained
- 1 teaspoon dried oregano
- 1 teaspoon dried thyme
- 1/2 teaspoon dried rosemary
- Salt and pepper to taste
- 4 cups fresh spinach, chopped
- Grated Parmesan cheese for serving (optional)

Instructions:

In a large pot or Dutch oven, heat the olive oil over medium heat. Add the Italian sausage, breaking it up with a spoon, and cook until browned. Remove any excess fat.

Add the chopped onion, minced garlic, carrots, and celery to the pot. Cook for about 5 minutes, or until the vegetables are softened.

Pour in the chicken broth, white beans, diced tomatoes (with their juice), oregano, thyme, rosemary, salt, and pepper. Stir to combine.

Bring the soup to a simmer, then reduce the heat to low. Let it simmer for about 20-25 minutes to allow the flavors to meld.

Add the chopped spinach to the pot and cook for an additional 5 minutes until the spinach wilts.

Taste the soup and adjust the seasoning if necessary.

Serve the Italian Sausage and White Bean Soup hot, garnished with grated Parmesan cheese if desired.

This soup is perfect for a comforting and filling meal. Enjoy!

Cucumber Avocado Salad

Ingredients:

- 2 large cucumbers, sliced
- 2 ripe avocados, diced
- 1/2 red onion, thinly sliced
- 1/4 cup fresh cilantro, chopped
- 2 tablespoons extra-virgin olive oil
- 1 tablespoon lime juice (or lemon juice)
- Salt and pepper to taste
- Optional: Red pepper flakes for a hint of spice

Instructions:

In a large bowl, combine the sliced cucumbers, diced avocados, thinly sliced red onion, and chopped cilantro.
In a small bowl, whisk together the extra-virgin olive oil and lime (or lemon) juice.
Season with salt and pepper to taste.
Pour the dressing over the cucumber and avocado mixture.
Toss the salad gently to coat the ingredients evenly with the dressing.
If desired, add a pinch of red pepper flakes for a bit of spice.
Let the salad sit for a few minutes to allow the flavors to meld.
Taste and adjust the seasoning if needed.
Serve the Cucumber Avocado Salad immediately as a refreshing side dish or a light meal.

Feel free to customize the salad by adding ingredients like cherry tomatoes, feta cheese, or grilled shrimp. This salad is not only delicious but also packed with nutrients. Enjoy!

Lemon Rosemary Grilled Chicken Thighs

Ingredients:

- 4-6 bone-in, skin-on chicken thighs
- 1/4 cup olive oil
- 3 tablespoons fresh lemon juice
- 2 tablespoons chopped fresh rosemary
- 3 cloves garlic, minced
- 1 teaspoon lemon zest
- Salt and pepper, to taste

Instructions:

In a bowl, whisk together the olive oil, lemon juice, chopped rosemary, minced garlic, lemon zest, salt, and pepper to create the marinade.

Place the chicken thighs in a large resealable plastic bag or a shallow dish.

Pour the marinade over the chicken, ensuring each piece is well coated. Seal the bag or cover the dish and let it marinate in the refrigerator for at least 30 minutes to allow the flavors to infuse into the chicken.

Preheat your grill to medium-high heat.

Remove the chicken from the marinade, allowing any excess to drip off.

Place the chicken thighs on the preheated grill, skin side down. Grill for about 6-8 minutes per side, or until the internal temperature reaches 165°F (74°C) and the chicken is cooked through.

During the last few minutes of grilling, you can baste the chicken with any remaining marinade for added flavor.

Once cooked, remove the chicken from the grill and let it rest for a few minutes before serving.

Garnish with additional fresh rosemary and lemon slices for a decorative touch.

These Lemon Rosemary Grilled Chicken Thighs pair well with a variety of side dishes, such as roasted vegetables, a fresh green salad, or even some couscous. Enjoy your delicious and aromatic grilled chicken thighs!

www.ingramcontent.com/pod-product-compliance
Lightning Source LLC
LaVergne TN
LVHW081611060526
838201LV00054B/2193